ANDREW YOUNG
A MATTER OF CHOICE

D1035304

Library of Congress Cataloging in Publication Data

Simpson, Janice Claire.
    Andrew Young: a matter of choice.

    (Headliners I)
    SUMMARY: A biography of the black congressman who
was appointed United States ambassador to the United Nations
in 1977.
        1. Young, Andrew J., 1932-   — Juvenile literature.   2.
Civil rights workers — United States — Biography — Juvenile
literature.   3. Ambassadors — United States — Biography —
Juvenile literature.   4. Legislators — United States — Biography
— Juvenile literature.   5. United States. Congress. House —
Biography — Juvenile literature.   [1. Young, Andrew J., 1932-
        2. Statesmen.   3. Afro-Americans — Biography]   I.
Title.   II. Series.
E840.8.Y64S55   327'.2'0924   [B] [92] 77-29229
ISBN 0-88436-472-0 lib. bdg.
ISBN 0-88436-473-9 pbk.

© 1978 by EMC Corporation
All Rights reserved. Published 1978

This work may not be transmitted by television
or other devices or processes or copies, recast,
transformed or adapted in any manner, in whole
or in part, except where permission is granted.

Published 1978. Produced by EMC Corporation
180 East Sixth Street, Saint Paul, Minnesota 55101
Printed in the United States of America
0 9 8 7 6 5 4 3 2 1

+
921
Yo8si

ANDREW YOUNG
A MATTER OF CHOICE

BY JAN SIMPSON

EMC CORPORATION ST. PAUL, MINNESOTA

It was about an hour before midnight when the handsome but weary young man climbed onto the stage at his campaign headquarters in downtown Atlanta.

"We did it. We won," he told his supporters gathered before him. "And I want to thank you. I want to thank you all."

There were all kinds of people in the crowd. Some were black welfare mothers and white auto assembly plant workers. Others were middle class black professionals and the sons and daughters of old, wealthy white Georgia families. They all roared their approval. Together, they had just helped elect Andrew Young, the first black congressman from the deep South in over 70 years.

For the new congressman, surrounded by family and close friends, it was a very special moment. He remembered all too well the bitter early days of the civil rights struggle. Then, blacks had to march and demonstrate for the right to enter such places through the front door. Many times local sheriffs chased the demonstrators away with vicious dogs. But today, he and the people who worked so hard in his campaign had proved that there was a new South and that its people could work together.

Ambassador Young (right) with his mother, Daisy, brother, Walter and father, Andrew, Sr. in 1949.

Andrew Jackson Young Jr. had spent nearly all of his life in the South. He was born on March 12, 1932 and grew up in the colorful city of New Orleans, Louisiana. Andrew Sr. was a dentist and his wife, Daisy, taught school. The Young family lived comfortably in a mostly white, middle class neighborhood. As a boy, Andy sang in the church choir, took French horn lessons and worked after school cleaning his father's office. He and his younger brother, Walter, played and made friends with the white children in the neighborhood. But every so often, there was trouble. Some of the meaner boys would get together and chase the Young brothers home, calling after them, "Niggers, niggers."

Finally, Dr. Young hired Eddie Brown, a professional boxer, to teach the boys how to defend themselves. Andy and Walter ran home less after that but Andy didn't like the solution. He thought there had to be a better way to deal with that kind of mindless hate.

Daisy Young taught her sons to read before they even started school. The early lessons made it easy for Andy to skip several grades. At just fifteen, he started at Dillard University, a small black college in New Orleans. The next year, wanting more independence from his family, he went off to Howard University, a well known school for blacks in Washington D.C. There, Andy majored in biology. But he spent much of his time competing in swim and track meets and partying at fraternity dances.

Andrew Young uses prayer and meditation often.

Then, the summer before his last year at Howard, Andy began to worry about his future. He wasn't sure he wanted to be a dentist like his father. He wasn't sure what he wanted to be. The confusion went away when Andy met a young missionary who was on his way to Africa. The young minister's concern for the world and his sincere determination to make it a better place for all people to live in impressed Andy. He liked the idea of making a contribution that might help improve the world. He decided to become a minister too, and applied to Hartford Theological Seminary.

At the Seminary, Andy read books by religious leaders and great thinkers from all over the world. The book he liked best, though, was by Mohandas Gandhi, an Indian, who had taught his people to use marches and strikes instead of guns and bullets in their fight for freedom from England. Gandhi called his non-violent philosophy "passive resistance." It was a way of life that Andy would come to know well.

In 1955, Andy graduated from the Seminary and applied for a missionary post in the African country of Angola. But the Portuguese officials who controlled Angola weren't admitting black missionaries into the country. Disappointed, Andy and his pretty new wife, Jean, returned to the South.

Andy Young's campaign included Coretta Scott King (left) and his wife Jean.

There, the Youngs prepared to settle down to the quiet life of a country preacher's family in Thomasville, Georgia. Jean taught school and they began their family. But in the late 1950s, a black Southern preacher's life was anything but quiet. More and more, black Southerners began to question the way things were done in the South. "Why do we have to sit at the back of the bus while whites ride comfortably in front?" they asked. "Why do we have to enter stores through side alley doors marked 'colored' while white customers walk easily through the front doors?" they wanted to know. Slowly, they began to protest for fair and equal treatment.

In 1966, Andy led protest marches and spoke at rallies such as this one at the state capitol in Jackson, Mississippi.

Many, including Andy and Jean Young, realized that voting was a strong weapon in the fight for equality. Few blacks in the South were registered to vote. Those who tried were often turned down when they failed to pass difficult voting tests. The Youngs began to talk to the people of their church about the importance of voting. Andy became president of a local group that began a voter registration drive.

For a while, things went well. Some people began to register to vote. Some of the older people had never tried to register before. They were eager to have a voice in government. Then the local chapter of the Ku Klux Klan, a group that hated blacks, began to threaten the people who went to register or even talked about voting. Some people were beaten. Others lost their jobs. Still, people continued to try and vote in Georgia and throughout the South.

Andy Young enjoys many moments with his family. Here he's pictured with his wife, his parents and three of his four children.

About three years later, the National Council of Churches asked Andy to join its staff in New York City. Andy was proud and pleased to receive the offer. But it was very hard for him to leave the South he loved, even with all its problems. He thought, perhaps making a different kind of contribution could be very important. After much prayer and thought, he and Jean and their two small daughters, Andrea and Lisa, moved to New York.

Andy was assigned the job of designing programs for young people. The work was interesting and the big city was exciting. Still, Andy continued to read about the marches and voter registration work in the South. He wrote to friends often, making suggestions and giving advice on how they should handle the problems.

One day, Martin Luther King, Jr., the husband of one of Jean's hometown friends, wrote Andy. The women had introduced their husbands earlier. Then, Rev. King had been organizing protestors in Montgomery, Alabama. Now, Rev. King was one of the biggest leaders in the civil rights movement.

Rev. King said he remembered how well Andy had worked in Thomasville. And he'd heard many of Andy's suggestions for new projects. He wondered if Andy would come to Atlanta and work with him and his group, SCLC, the Southern Christian Leadership Conference. Would he? It was just what Andy had been waiting for. The Young family returned South again.

Finally, Andy had found his mission, a way to
make his contribution. The young minister worked
long hard hours. He liked getting up early. It gave him
more time to do all the things he wanted to do. Andy
marched and sang freedom songs like "We Shall
Overcome." He organized sit-ins and voter
registration drives.

Once, when a group of protestors marched around the old slave market in St. Augustine, Florida, an angry bystander grabbed Andy and beat him with a stick. The policemen just stood and watched. Andy didn't fight back. He remembered the teachings of Mohandas Gandhi. He knew there were other ways to win the struggle for equality.

Because he'd lived with whites in New Orleans, studied with them in Hartford and worked with them in New York, Andy knew that there were also white people who were interested in equality for all people. As he moved from city to city with the other protestors, Andy searched for those understanding whites. When he found them, he'd ask them for their support and influence in helping blacks to get jobs that were only open to whites or to be allowed to eat in restaurants that refused to serve them.

Andy was good, too, at talking with those whites who didn't want to see the old ways change. He often came up with good compromises, things that made the changes easier for them to bear.

Gradually, Rev. King began to depend more and more on Andy's ability to handle bargaining problems and even to settle small arguments among the protestors themselves. Rev. King appointed Andy one of his top aides and chose him to help write the Voting Rights Act that made it easier for black people to vote. Andy also had a part in writing the Civil Rights Act that made it easier for blacks to get a good education and better jobs.

KAUKAUNA PUBLIC LIBRARY
Kaukauna, Wis.

Often, the wise leader would insist that Andy leave a demonstration when the police appeared and began to make arrests. Andy's cool reasoning was far more valuable outside than his body would be inside a jail, Rev. King would explain.

Andy had lots of "important" support in his campaign, including Rev. Ralph Abernathy (left, back) and Julian Bond (right, front).

The more they worked together, the closer the two men became. Often, when they were alone, driving from a march in one city to a demonstration in another, the two would munch graham crackers and sing old church hymns or tell silly jokes. Sometimes, they'd share the dreams each had for his children.

On April 4, 1968, Rev. King, Andy and some of the other top SCLC aides spent the whole day in a meeting in a room in the Lorraine Motel in Memphis, Tennessee. The men had come to Memphis to help the black sanitation workers. The workers had been striking for three months to get higher pay and better working conditions.

After the meeting, many of them including Rev. King, went out on the balcony for some fresh air. It was a cool evening and one of the aides told Rev. King that he should get his coat before they went out to dinner. As Rev. King turned to get his coat, a shot rang out. At first, the men thought it was a firecracker. Then they saw Rev. King fall against the wall holding his head. And they saw the blood running down his shirt. Two of them ran to him. One, Rev. Ralph Abernathy, cradled the wounded man's head in his lap. The other, Andy, felt for his pulse to see if he were still alive. An ambulance came quickly but shortly after Rev. King arrived at the hospital, he was dead.

Andy's interest in Africa is longstanding. It was almost natural for him to become U.S. Ambassador to the United Nations.

One of Ambassador Young's first steps was to visit Africa. Here he meets with the President of Mozambique, Samora Machel.

Andy stayed on with SCLC for a while after Rev. King's death, but he missed the sense of purpose and direction his friend had given the group.

By 1970, black people began to realize that having the vote wasn't enough. They had to use that voting power to elect black officials who knew their needs, who would speak for them and help make policy that would give them those things.

In Atlanta, the old freedom fighters gathered together to choose a candidate to run for the seat in the 5th Congressional District. The man who held the seat was Fletcher Thompson, a white southerner of the old school who rarely even visited the black neighborhoods in his district. He was a good target but the group couldn't decide who should run against him.

Some suggested Coretta Scott King, Martin's widow. She was well known and could possibly win some of the more liberal white votes, they said. Others thought Ralph Abernathy, the new president of SCLC, was a good choice. Still others wanted Julian Bond, the good-looking young state representative. Bond had won national recognition at the last Democratic convention when he was nominated for Vice President. Slowly, more and more people mentioned Andy. His skill at working successfully with both blacks and whites was needed, they agreed.

But this wasn't the only group thinking about someone black to run in the 5th District. Some others wanted Lonnie King, a well-known civil rights worker. The two black men were forced to campaign against each other. Andy won the Democratic primary. But, he was not able to get the white support he needed to win the general election. Many whites did not want to vote for a black, at all.

Two years later, Andy was ready. He convinced the black and white community that he was the best candidate. His district boundaries were also changed. It meant that there weren't so many conservative whites voting for or against him. He won the primary easily.

WITHDRAWN
From The Kaukauna Public Library

This time, however, Andy's Republican opponent was Rodney Cook. He was a moderate white. He also had a great deal of money. Cook could afford many more TV commercials than Andy. Some people thought Cook might win just because so many people began to recognize his name.

But Andy worked hard. He visited black church socials in the city's poor Buttermilk Bottom area. And he went to white tea parties in the richer areas of the city. His supporters went door to door, asking people to vote for Andy. They covered the district with posters that told voters to "Think Young" or to choose "Young Ideas" for Congress.

A few weeks before the election, the courts ordered busing to integrate the Atlanta school system. Many people thought the unpopular decision would cost Andy votes. But the skillful politician managed to stay clear of any trouble on the issue.

Election day was rainy and cold. The candidates were afraid that the bad weather would keep the voters home. But 65 percent of the black vote went to Andy. Some of them had to get up extra early and vote before they went to work. Others walked long distances to the polls, because they didn't have cars. They all remembered that Andy had worked hard to give them the right to vote. They wanted to show him that they were grateful.

Victory for Andy Young, when he ran for Congress. In the background, Maynard Jackson, Mayor of Atlanta and Representative Julian Bond.

Whites voted for Andy, too. They believed him when he said that he planned to work for better jobs, better education and better health care—things that would help both black and white people in Atlanta. More whites voted for him than had ever voted for a black candidate before. Together, black and white voters sent Andy Young to Congress.

In Washington, Andy plunged right in. Just as he'd promised the people who voted for him, Andy's bills weren't "black bills" but people bills. They were things that black people needed and they were things all people wanted, too.

Andy Young with his youngest daughter, Paula.

Andy also became active in foreign affairs. He attended meetings in Germany and Japan and he visited Africa often. During one trip, he met Robert Sobukwe, one of the black South African fighters for equality. The two men became friends. Andy later took two of Sobukwe's children home to live with the Young family. It now included another daughter, Paula, and a son, Andrew Jackson Young, III. The family called him Bo.

The new congressman quickly earned the respect of his co-workers. "Andy Young is a man of his word. He keeps his promises," they said. "He knows when to give in and when to stay and fight," they told one another. Sometimes, Andy did unpopular things. He was the only member of the congressional Black Caucus to vote to approve Gerald Ford as Vice President.

But even Western and Northern black congressman who thought Andy could be a bit more militant, agreed that he was a very good policymaker. The people in the 5th District agreed too. Even some of the businessmen who had been reluctant to support Andy at first, agreed that he was a fair man. They knew that he would speak honestly for them and that others would listen to him when he spoke. Andy easily won re-election.

Andy Young during a casual moment with President Carter.

One of Andy's earliest white supporters was an elderly white woman named Lillian Carter. She contributed money to the Young campaign. She also told the candidate that he should meet her son, Jimmy. "You'd like each other," she said.

Jimmy Carter was running for governor of Georgia. He and Andy met for the first time at a political fund-raiser. But Carter didn't make much of an impression that night. Then, one day, Carter went into Pascal's, a popular hang-out for Atlanta's black politicians, to ask for support. After the candidate finished talking to the politicians in the dining room, he went into the kitchen and chatted just as comfortably with the cooks and dishwashers, asking them for their support too.

Andy Young's support was invaluable to Jimmy Carter during his campaign for President.

Andy watched Carter's ease in talking to both groups. He'd always liked a man who talked to the little people and the well known ones. Andy also watched when, as governor, Carter appointed more blacks to positions on various state offices and agencies than ever before.

Andy was still a little nervous about putting too much faith in a white, southern-born, country-raised politician. But he knew it was time for the South to speak with a new voice. The time had passed for the South to be represented any longer by George Wallace, the governor of Alabama, who had fought so hard against the civil rights movement. Andy looked around at some of the other new, liberal governors in the South like Reuben Askew of Florida and Dale Bumpers of Arkansas. Slowly he decided that perhaps Lillian Carter was right. There was something likeable about her son.

Jimmy Carter had been watching Andy Young, too. He saw how fairly Andy approached problems and he saw how easily Andy gained the respect of those he worked with. Early in 1974, before he announced his plans to run for president, Carter asked Andy to join his strategy team. Andy agreed. He became the first nationally known public person to support the candidate that many people jokingly called "Jimmy Who?" because so few of them had ever heard of him before.

Andy's help was important throughout the campaign. He persuaded black leaders and white liberals to support Jimmy Carter, although many of them were worried about the idea of a Southerner for President. He advised the candidate to apologize after he used the words "ethnic purity" in a remark that angered many voters. Often, Andy was called to Carter's home in Plains, Georgia, and asked to go over Carter's speeches before the candidate gave them. Andy also helped Carter decide to support a national health insurance plan that would make it easier for all people in the United States to afford good medical care. He urged the candidate to support the black majority in South Africa who wanted freedom from the white people who ruled them. Finally, as chairman of the Democratic Party's voter registration drive, Andy used all of his old skills to get out the vote among the blacks and other poor people in the big cities. He knew they would support Jimmy Carter.

Andy worked hard and he expected Carter to keep the promises he'd made to the voters. But he didn't ask for any rewards for himself. "I don't want any fancy new positions. I want to stay in Congress," he told friends. Andy even gave up the chance to nominate Jimmy Carter for President at the Democratic convention in New York, when Peter Rodino, another congressman, asked for the honor. But after the election, Jimmy Carter told the reporters he owed his success to one man—Andy Young.

President Carter made the post of U.S. Ambassador to the U.N. a cabinet level job. Here are cabinet members Andrew Young, Charles Schultz and Zbigniew Brzezinski.

Andy meant it when he said he didn't want any position in the new President's cabinet. But Jimmy Carter had other ideas. He knew that the post of United Nations Ambassador was becoming more and more important. The poor countries of the world in Africa, Asia and Latin America were beginning to accuse the large, wealthier nations—especially the United States—of not caring about them. The President knew that he would need a United Nations Ambassador who could talk easily with the representatives from all the countries and convince them that the United States still wanted to help them. He also knew that Andy Young was perfect for the job.

Jimmy Carter wouldn't take no for an answer. He called again. He called Jean Young too. Would she put in a good word for him with her husband, the President asked. Cyrus Vance, the new Secretary of State, called Andy too. "Sure hope you're going to stay on the team," he said.

But when Andy's old civil rights friends heard about the offer, they called and begged him not to take it. The United Nations job wasn't important enough, some told him. Others warned him that many older and wiser politicians had ruined their careers by accepting the U.N. job.

Ambassador Young and wife Jean at inauguration party.

Finally, Andy went home and locked himself in his study. He fasted to clear his mind. He prayed for guidance to make the right decision. Several thoughts went through his mind as he sat there alone.

Secretary General of the United Nations, Kurt Waldheim at center as President Carter and Andrew Young sign United Nations Human Rights bills.

Ambassador Young, first black to hold position of U.S. Ambassador to the United Nations, faced many difficulties when he first started his job.

In 1967, he and Martin King had marched in front of the United Nations to protest against the war in Vietnam. It seemed strange to think that he might be an ambassador, where he had once led protests. He also remembered Dr. Ralph Bunche, the first black man to win the Nobel Prize for Peace. Dr. Bunche had helped to start the United Nations. He had also been one of the first black leaders Andy had admired when he was still a young student. Then, he thought about the freedom struggle in Africa. He remembered his old wish to work for a better life for the people on that continent. Here was a chance to make a contribution. Andy knew he couldn't turn it down.

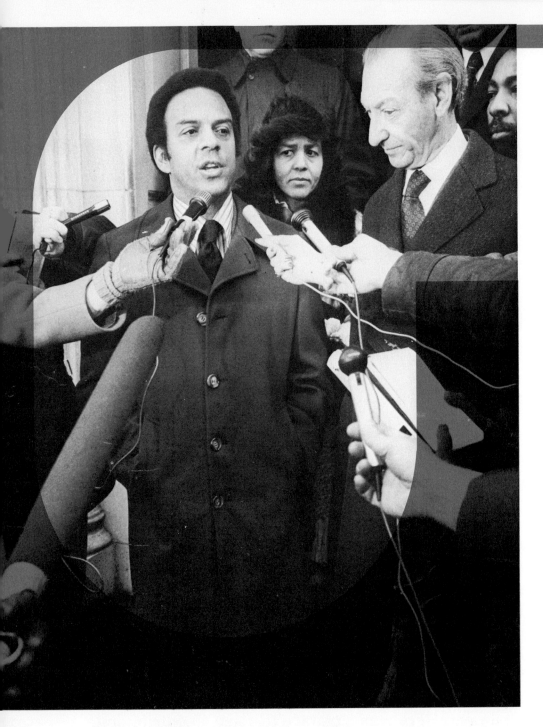

Because of Andy's stand on human rights in Africa, he was called many cruel nicknames.

African leaders, such as Kenneth Kaunda, President of Zambia (seated, left) respected Andy from the start.

He called the President. "I'll take the job," he told him. "But there's one condition. I've got to be free to speak my mind, to say what I feel even if it disagrees with the way you see things, Mr. President." The President agreed. Andrew Jackson Young, Jr. became the highest ranking black policy maker in American history.

African leaders throughout the continent all welcomed the new ambassador warmly. The leaders knew of Andy's past fights against inequality in his own country. And they knew of his personal friendship with Jimmy Carter. They felt that Andy Young would present their stories fairly to the American people and their new President.

All over Africa, Ambassador Young was greeted with great respect.

But back at home in the United States, the newspapers and some old government officials were criticizing the new ambassador. In Rhodesia, Andy had talked with the freedom fighters there as well as with the white government officials. He said he wanted to get the whole story. The newspapers and officials said he shouldn't have talked to the rebel freedom fighters. At a reception in South Africa, Andy joined a group of performing dancers. The people were pleased that he felt so at ease with them. But at home, people said that such behavior wasn't dignified enough for an ambassador.

Even though many people did not understand Ambassador Young's message, he continued to speak out.

The biggest problem, however, came up every time Andy talked about racism. The white South Africans wouldn't allow the black people in that country to participate in government. They were just as bad as the whites who had tried to keep blacks out of the schools and stores in the South, Andy said. Many people said that such talk would make the South African government mad. They began to call Andy by the cruel nickname "Motor Mouth."

Jimmy Carter continued to stand by his friend, but all the talk still hurt. Andy couldn't help wondering if he were doing the right things. Then, he remembered how hard it had been to win equality in the South. Those freedom fighters had been called mean names too. Maybe some of the things he said weren't pleasant to hear. Still they had to be said. How could the wrongs ever be changed if people didn't know about them?

Andy knew he had no choice. He had to continue to speak out against those he believed to be wrong no matter how hard it was.

Andy's judgment proved to be right. In just six months, diplomats from around the world began to praise Andrew Young. The news media began to say that he was doing a good job. People began to understand that Andy could really help as an international peacemaker, especially in Africa.

It was a matter of choice.

Andy worked as a member of the U.S. Cabinet and on the National Security Council. Wherever he went, he worked for non-violent ways of solving problems. His beliefs didn't make things easy for him. But for Andrew Young, doing what he believes is a matter of choice.

PHOTO CREDITS

Freelance Photographers: page 31
Sygma: Owen Franken pages 33 and 39
      Bill Campbell pages 8, 36, and 37
      Ken Hawkins pages 27 and 28
      J.P. Laffont pages 18, 19 and 20
Wide World: pages 26 and 35
Courtesy of Jean and Andrew Young: pages 6, 10, 12, 14, 16, 23 and 24

EMC wishes to thank Ambassador Young, his wife Jean and their
staff for their cooperation in making this reader possible.